T0131956

A Tiny Step Forward

Charlene Khaghan & Jill Starishevsky

Archway Publishing books may be ordered through booksellers or by contacting:

Archway Publishing
1663 Liberty Drive
Bloomington, IN 47403
www.archwaypublishing.com
1 (888) 242-5904

ISBN: 978-1-4808-6626-3 (sc)
ISBN: 978-1-4808-6624-9 (hc)
ISBN: 978-1-4808-6625-6 (e)

Print information available on the last page.

Archway Publishing rev. date: 7/2/2019

For my five amazing children –

Max, James, Remi, Steven and Victoria

who lovingly remember their father

and show strength and resilience every day.

Dear Reader,

If you have picked up this book, chances are you or someone close to you has suffered a loss. I, too, once lost someone close to me. When I was 42-years-old, I came home from a day at the zoo with my five children to find my husband had suddenly passed away. Not only was I forced to reckon with my own shock and acceptance, I also knew I had to find ways to help my children deal with their own reactions in the days and years to come.

After much time spent reading, talking and soul-searching, I've come to understand the importance of finding happiness in our lives despite the losses we go through. Although we may encounter reminders of our lost ones at any time, there is a lot to gain from not trying to push away the thoughts and feelings this triggers. Rather, by embracing the memories we have of this person, we can find a renewed sense of strength and joy in ourselves. It is with this understanding that I wrote this book, in the hopes of helping those going through a similar situation as my family and I once did.

The purpose of this book is to let young children know that if they have lost someone close, be it a friend or family member, it is okay to feel upset and to miss this person as they grieve; then, as life begins to move on, it is okay to once again feel *happy* and to enjoy life, as their loved one would have wanted for them. Though each day may only be a tiny step forward, my hope is that the final stanza of this book will always remind readers that our loved ones are never truly gone as long as they live on in our hearts.

Yours,

Charlene Khaghan

Charlene Khaghan

Sad things happen, as they sometimes do.

I never thought something this sad could happen to me and you.

I really, really miss you since you passed away.

For a very long time, that was hard for me to say.

It has taken me a while to make some sense of it all,

Learning to deal with new feelings, whether big or small.

I feel angry, I feel sad, I just want to yell out WHY?

But slowly after time, I'm learning how to get by.

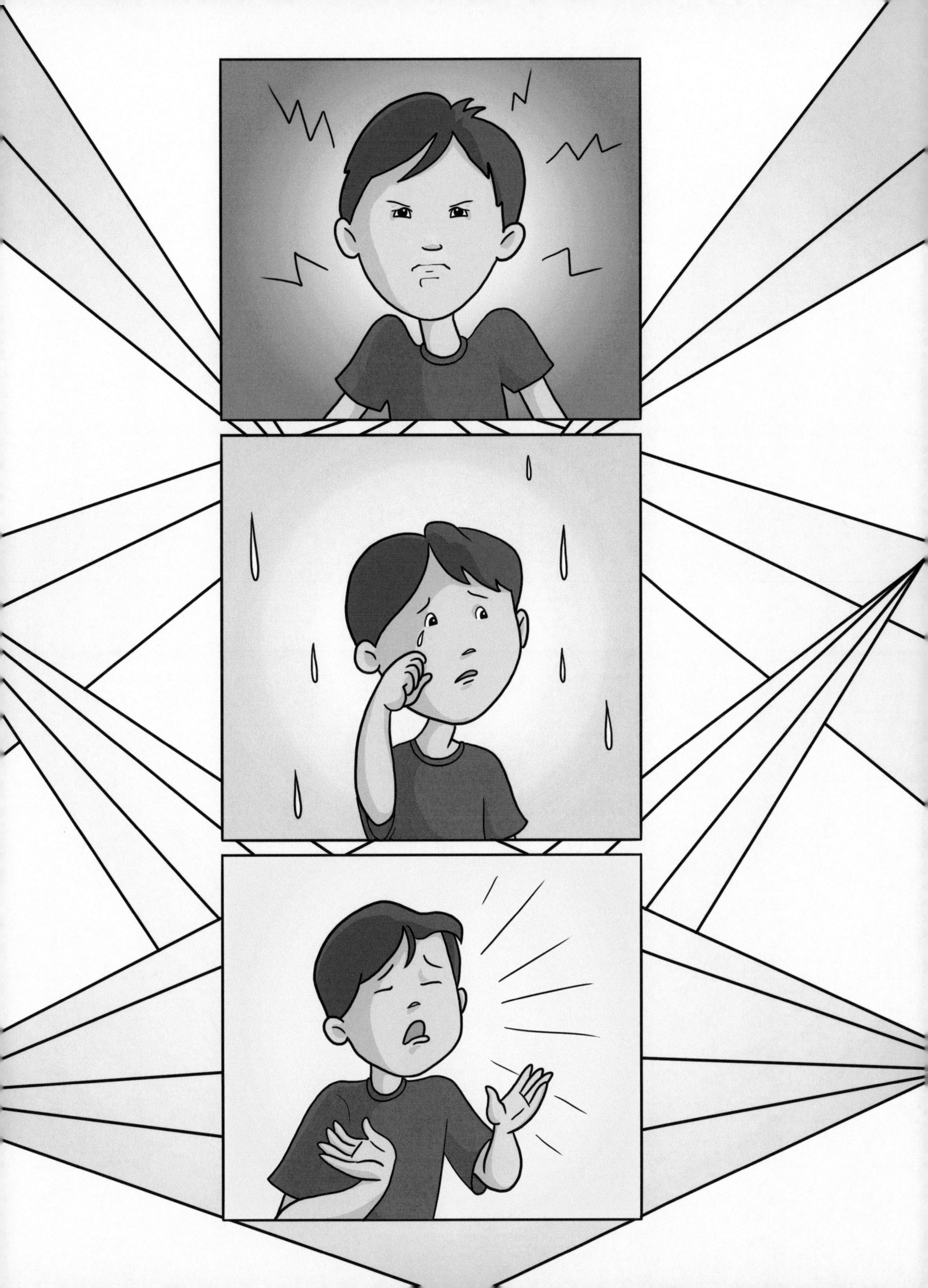

I take a tiny step forward to feel happy as can be,

Knowing in my heart, that's what you'd want for me.

I know you always loved me and hold that thought so dear,

As I remember our special times, all throughout the year.

This morning when I woke up and stretched my arms in the air,

I got out of bed, brushed my teeth and decided what to wear.

“Have a good day at school,” you always used to say,

Thoughts of you pop into mind every single day.

Last week was a holiday, at services there was a crowd,

The family sat close together and said our prayers aloud.

In the quiet little moments, I wish you could be there,

I was warmed by the thought of you and times we used to share.

This Saturday was sunny and we were at the game,

Although we had lots of fun it wasn't quite the same.

We cheered so loud and jumped around and gave some high fives too,

In that instant you crossed my mind and I could picture you.

I fell down at the park and really skinned my knee,

It hurt so much I wanted to cry, but was brave as I could be.

I remembered how you kissed my boo boos and made them go away,

I picked myself up, brushed myself off and headed back to play.

Last month was my birthday and all my friends were there,

Chocolate cake and presents and laughter we did share.

“You’re getting to be SO big,” I imagined you to say,

I smiled as I thought of you on my special day.

This summer I made a sandcastle, almost as big as me,

I jumped the waves and collected shells I found along the sea.

I had such fun in the sand and laughed the whole day through,

A day with friends and family reminded me of you.

We sat around the dinner table, chatting about our day,

Sharing stories, passing dishes, all had something to say.

I tried my best at school and even learned something new,

I was proud of myself today and know you would have been too.

At night when I get into bed and pull the blankets up tight,

I think of how you stroked my hair and made me feel just right.

There's a special place in my heart for the memories that I keep,

I tenderly remember you before I fall asleep.

I tell myself it will be okay, we will help each other through,

There's not a day that passes that I don't think of you.

And when I want to tell someone that you are on my mind,

I draw a heart around my heart and you're never hard to find.

Thoughts and Memories:

Printed in the United States
By Bookmasters